JUST
CAUSE

1998-99 NWMS READING BOOKS

RESOURCE BOOK FOR THE LEADER

IMAGINE THE HARVEST
Edited by Beverlee Borbe

FOR THE READER

AGAINST THE TIDE
The Miracle of Growth in the Netherlands
By Cisca Verwoerd

DAUGHTER OF AFRICA
The Story of Juliet Ndzimandze
By Charles Gailey

JUST CAUSE
How Nazarene Students Are Changing Their World
By Frank Moore

PLACES CALLED INDIA
By Tim Crutcher

PREACHER WITH A MISSION
The Story of Nina Griggs Gunter
By Helen Temple

WINDOWS TO ALBANIA
By Connie Griffith Patrick

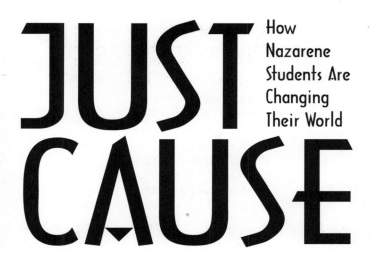

JUST CAUSE

How
Nazarene
Students Are
Changing
Their World

FRANK MOORE

Nazarene Publishing House
Kansas City, Missouri

This book is in memory of my late colleague and friend, Charles Morrow, who was a personification of the philosophy and goals of C.A.U.S.E. To this day his fingerprints remain on everything we do with C.A.U.S.E.

Contents

Preface 9

Acknowledgments 11

1. The Great Adventure 13

2. From Smallville to the Jungle 25

3. A Compass Without a Needle 33

4. Cat Guarding the Parakeets 46

5. He with the Most Toys Wins 56

6. It Keeps Going and Going and Going 69

7. The Big Picture 83

In Memoriam 93

Appendix 95

Notes 96

Frank Moore is professor of theology and serves as chair of the Division of Religion and Philosophy at MidAmerica Nazarene University, Olathe, Kansas. He has been at MNU for 13 years. His wife, Sue, also teaches at MNU. They have been the campus coordinators of C.A.U.S.E. since its inception. Frank and Sue have one son, Brent, a sophomore at MNU.

Preface

The stories of people and projects in this book come from a program in the Church of the Nazarene called C.A.U.S.E. C.A.U.S.E. is an acronym for College and University students Serving and Enabling. It is a unique short-term program involving college students in ministry around the world. The program is coordinated through International Headquarters for the Church of the Nazarene in Kansas City. They select one particular mission field each year and attempt to make an impact in an area of extreme need.

My wife and I both teach at MidAmerica Nazarene University, and we've been involved with C.A.U.S.E. since its inception. In the next few pages, I want to share a little of the story of C.A.U.S.E. with you. The neat thing about this story is that the central characters are not missionaries, college professors, pastors, or general church leaders. The central figures are average, ordinary young people who are trying to find themselves and their place in the world. They love music and junk food. They hate pimples and being bored. They love adventure and a thrilling challenge. They also love the Lord, and they're ready to jump in and lend a hand in His work. The bigger the challenge and the tougher the assignment, the quicker they dive in and get involved.

Here is your chance to join them.

Frank Moore

Acknowledgments

A special thanks goes to the following:

1. Sue, my wife, for her undying support over the past 12 years of work trips. She has shared the team sponsorship load and worked quietly behind the scenes to make each trip a success and each student a valued member of the team.

2. Allen and Madeline Tollefson, building contractors, who have traveled with every team since 1988. We greatly appreciate their invaluable contribution of new clothes, shoes, and Bibles to each project.

3. Missionaries Duane Rensberry, Jim Johnson, Craig and Gail Zickefoose, Marty Hoskins, and Jim Cooper for providing updated information from the field for use in this book. Tim Mastin, Gustavo Crocker, and Steve Weber of International Headquarters provided updates from their perspectives.

4. Home churches, family, and friends of student team members who assisted in raising support and donating supplies and medicine for each project.

5. Each team member who sacrificed and gave so freely to mission work. The Spirit of God used their youthful energy and enthusiasm to accomplish great things for His kingdom.

Chapter 1

The Great Adventure

WE'RE GOING TO DIE right here on top of this mountain!" I exclaimed to my wife, Sue, as I looked out the airplane window. Our plane had suddenly dropped its left wing and started sliding out of the sky—sideways. Everything shifted to our side of the plane. Everyone sitting around us had a look of panic in their eyes as the ground was fast approaching our left windows. By the time the plane leveled out, its wing tip had almost hit the trees on the rugged mountaintop.

No sooner did we catch our breath from that ordeal than we felt the bottom fall out from under us like a roller coaster on its first big drop. Our plane entered another dive, this time nose first. Sue grabbed my arm and held on for dear life. "We are all going to die right here on the side of this mountain," she cried in terror. "We'll never make it to the ground in one piece."

The day had started routinely enough. We loaded our team of 23 college students and our luggage onto a Continental Airlines flight from Kansas City to New Orleans. We changed planes in New

Orleans and headed down to Tegucigalpa [tuh-goo-suh-GAHL-puh], Honduras, on Tan Sahsa. That's where we made our mistake. There's nothing routine about Tan Sahsa or the flight to Honduras.

You've probably never heard of Tan Sahsa. Neither had we until that day. It's a relatively small Central American commercial airline. Even though we didn't know anything about it, we figured it must be safe. After all, it made daily flights to the United States and hadn't been exposed for safety violations on the evening news.

Excitement built as we prepared to board the Boeing 727 jet. We should have suspected that we were dealing with a different breed of airline when the counter agent matter-of-factly told us our late flight was always a couple of hours behind schedule. But our plane finally pulled into the gate from Tegucigalpa and was serviced for the return trip, so we didn't think any more about it. The flight attendant gave the boarding call, and we walked down the jet way and right into the twilight zone.

Words cannot describe the sight that greeted us as we stepped aboard that vintage plane! But it was too late to turn back. A rubber mat instead of carpet covered the floor. Holes in the seat fabric exposed large wads of foam stuffing. It looked as if an entire neighborhood of stray cats had sharpened their claws on the seat backs, and the seat fabric came from a long-forgotten era.

There was no use in the flight attendants making an announcement to put our seat backs and tray tables in their original upright and locked po-

sition. Several seats lay permanently limp in a reclining position, and tray tables hung collapsed from seat backs throughout the plane without a latch to lock.

Instead of overhead storage compartments, rope netting hung from the ceiling for small carryons. The plane walls were held in place with clothes hanger wires pulled through holes in the wall, twisted, and bent to one side. Don't even ask about the toilet paper covering the rest room floor.[1]

"We're all going to die in this old thing," I told Sue. "Thankfully I won't be around to try and explain why we didn't turn around and get off." I saw we only had one possible hope—to pray for guardian angels. That's exactly what I did as we taxied out to the runway.

We learned on the runway that our pilots were either daredevils, thrill seekers, or rejected operators of amusement park rides. What a takeoff! We shot into the sky like a bottle rocket! I think our pilots accidentally got the takeoff plans for the Space Shuttle. I have never seen such a look of horror as I saw on my team's faces.

Eventually our nerves settled from the takeoff, and we enjoyed our delicious lunch of rice, beans, and fried bananas. We even settled back and dozed for a while. Then the intercom cracked to life with an announcement, first in Spanish, then in very poor English. I didn't catch much of what came over the decrepit speakers, but I did hear the word "Tegucigalpa," so I assumed it was time to prepare for landing.

Like they say, "What goes up must co. down." In our case make that "fall out of the sky sideways." Tegucigalpa lies in a deep valley, completely surrounded by mountains. From the air it looks like a city at the bottom of a large volcano—something right out of an old James Bond movie. Pilots have a special challenge maneuvering planes through the glide path to the ground. First, they must clear the mountaintop, then drop into the valley for the runway like a dive-bomber. We cleared the mountain with what appeared to be only a few feet to spare. That's when my nerves completely unraveled, and I strongly wished I had just stayed in bed that day. But I hadn't, and now I felt responsible for the safety of my wife and our college students as we quickly approached the ground. There was only one thing left to do—PRAY HARD. I did, and God helped us get on the ground in one piece.

I didn't figure anyone would believe us when we told them about our Tan Sahsa flight, but they did. Apparently, a favorite pastime in that part of Central America is exchanging stories of takeoffs and landings at Tegucigalpa with Tan Sahsa. We told our story to everyone who would listen. Our friends later showed us gruesome newspaper pictures of a boy killed a week earlier by a jet's wheels hitting him in the head as he played on the very mountain we had just flown over.

Missionaries Duane and Linda Rensberry, Mike and Kathy Robinson, and Dana Benscoter met us at the Tegucigalpa International Airport with members from our work site at November 30

Church of the Nazarene. The community was named November 30 because it was officially recognized by the government as a settlement on that date. The members waved a large banner welcoming us. Their hearts and smiles were warmer than the tropical evening air we stepped into as we left the plane. We immediately felt their love.

The bus ride through the streets of Tegucigalpa presented more poverty than any of us had ever seen. We soon reached our church home for the week. It had all of the accommodations for housing our team. We slept on the floor on foam mats, and we cooked our meals in the church kitchen. It was like camping but without the bears, though we did see lots of bugs, spiders, and lizards. The guys soon found a basketball goal, so they were ready to unpack and stay. A tall wrought-iron fence and an around-the-clock guard protected the property. We felt safe.

Sunday brought church services, a tour of the work site, and a lot of sweat in the tropical heat. Monday was our first workday. The team jumped right in. Some already knew how to lay tin roofing, pour concrete, or build window frames. Missionaries Duane, Mike, and Dana conducted instruction for those who needed to learn. In no time, everyone fell in-line at a task. The work was hard, but we had the time of our lives as we lost ourselves in compassionate service. We found ways to make a game out of everything, and the hot, tedious work became fun.

The missionaries had never hosted an entire

team of college students before, so they hadn't seen anything like us. We laughed, joked, and played pranks on each other and the local helpers all day long. The guys chased the girls with strange looking bugs and lizards, and the screams rang out for blocks. Water fights occasionally broke out. Concrete found its way all over workers' backsides. Some of the team members took turns playing and practicing their Spanish with a large group of community kids attracted to the Americans. They learned each child's name, and soon every child within walking distance found our work site. We could hardly work for the swarm of kids outside the churchyard.

I went with most of the team to the work site each morning while Sue and a few girls prepared three meals a day in the church kitchen. Preparing three meals a day for 30 people in a small church kitchen provided its own challenges, but the cooks prepared great feasts. Of course, we were so hungry at the end of the day we would have eaten anything.

The week of construction gave us a few complications and a lot of laughs. One day Terry, one of the team members, announced, "I just stepped on a nail, but you don't need to worry. I walked down the hill to the river and washed my foot." He washed his foot in the river? That's the worst thing he could have done! Entire herds of livestock stand in the middle of that river to cool themselves, get away from the flies, and get a drink. Women beat their clothes on the rocks as they wash them and hang them on the bushes and shrubs to dry. Adults and children jump in with bars of soap and take daily baths. Ground sewage from the open sewer ditches of the surrounding villages drained into it. If that's not enough, little green things float all over the surface. It's a miracle Terry's foot didn't fall right off in that polluted river.

Another team member, Jack, had feet with built-in radar for freshly poured concrete. Just about every hour someone shouted, "Jack, get out of the concrete." Sure enough, he had wandered on to a new pour and left his footprints as a lasting reminder of his visit to Honduras. We all laughed about it and repaired the concrete. Jack was a great sport and a hard worker.

Sue and the girls at the kitchen had a scare one day. Dry weeds and trash covered the open fields near our home-base church, and somehow the weeds had caught fire. Flames of fire grew quite large in no time. They surrounded the church building and filled the windows in every direction with smoke. Sue and the others had to lay on the floor with their noses covered until the winds eventually cleared the building. Thankfully the church building was spared, and no one got sick from the smoke.

Our favorite activity was talking with the missionaries at the end of the day. They put a great deal of extra time and effort into our college team. They knew each team member by name and something about each one's personal life. They even took time to talk one-on-one about the way God was working in their own lives. They were great role models and examples for all of us. We could tell they wanted to expose us to missions so God could speak to us about His direction for our lives, our values, and His will for our futures.

Days brought work in the hot sun, and evenings brought church services—lots of church services. We soon learned that Honduran Nazarenes have some form of public worship every night of the week. So we came home from work, ate, cleaned up, and went to church most evenings. We participated in worship, sang Spanish songs, and gave testimonies. Fellowship times after service with the church people gave locals and us an opportunity to practice a few words of English or Spanish. We mostly used sign language, smiled, and pointed a lot. We formed friendships that will be renewed in heaven someday.

After we returned to our sleeping quarters in the evening, our team usually sat around and talked for a while. This gave us an opportunity to let down our hair, spend quality time together, and really get to know each other personally. Bedtime always brought lots of laughing, pranking, and threats to "get the lights out or else." An all-student work team differs a little from an adult church team. Students have tons of energy and active imaginations. So, we also spent part of our time together dodging water balloons, thawing out frozen underwear, and belching warm sodas.

The trip impacted all of us in more ways than just work and fun, however. By the middle of the week, I found myself in the midst of a personal cri-

Boarding Tan Sahsa for the trip home from Honduras

sis of heart. Even though I'd been raised in one of the poorest areas of the United States, I had never seen so much poverty and need in my entire life. Tuesday night I couldn't sleep. Pictures of my surroundings kept running through my mind. Pictures of little naked children playing in the open sewers. Pictures of kids digging through the trash, looking for something to eat. I cried most of the night as I tried to figure out how things had gone so badly wrong for so many people and what I might do to help. I didn't come to any conclusions that restless Tuesday night, but I determined I would do my best to get involved in some way to help.

Almost as quickly as it started, the week ended. We looked forward to getting back home, but not to another roller-coaster ride on Tan Sahsa. But since they were the only airline with service to New

Orleans, we had no choice. However, we weren't as afraid this time. Experiencing Tan Sahsa was part of experiencing a new culture. We'd experienced a lot of new foods, sights, customs, bugs, and smells that week. Why not one more Tan Sahsa ride? Sadness filled all of our hearts, and tears filled our eyes as we sat on the plane and looked back toward the airport. There stood Duane, Mike, Dana, and our new friends from the November 30 Church—all waving good-bye to us. We left a part of our hearts at the airport that day.

We soon learned why the Honduran pilots use a Space Shuttle takeoff. They must clear the steep mountain range surrounding Tegucigalpa, and the only way out is nearly straight up! So, up we went. We were soon munching on another plate of rice and beans with fried bananas. God protected us, and we returned to New Orleans without incident.

As soon as we cleared customs and immigration in New Orleans, we kissed the American soil—literally got down on our hands and knees and kissed the ground. We were never so glad to see an American flag and a picture of the president of the United States, and we seriously needed a junk food fix! No more fried bananas, rice, beans, and warm cola drinks for us. One thought controlled our collective minds: McDonald's. So, we walked a mile and a half to satisfy our high-cholesterol craving. We ate enough hamburgers, french fries, apple pies, and ice-cream sundaes to feed a small army. Come to think of it, we *were* a small army—for the Lord. One more plane ride brought us back to Kansas

City. We had been to another world, and no doubt, none of us would ever be the same.

Neither Sue nor I had any thoughts at the moment of doing another work trip. This was a one-shot deal as far as we both were concerned. But, soon after our return home, the evaluations from the missionaries and International Headquarters arrived. Everyone said the same thing, "College students have a lot to offer the mission field." They welcomed us back and encouraged teams from every Nazarene college and university to come as often as they could.

So we had to decide what to do next. The people at International Headquarters decided they could select a needy world area each year and coordinate an effort to involve all of the Nazarene colleges and universities. They needed an individual to spearhead, organize, and carry out the unified effort. This individual had to work with both the mission field and all of the Nazarene colleges and universities. He or she would need to travel to the project sight and make all arrangements, then go down again to stay with all of the teams as they worked. And most importantly, this person would work for free! The person who filled the bill in every way was Charles Morrow, agrimissions teacher at MidAmerica Nazarene University.

Charles coordinated the work of C.A.U.S.E. for two years. Then on October 21, 1989, Charles was preparing for that next trip, which meant going through Tegucigalpa, where we had been a little over three years before. But Charles wasn't as fortunate in his approach to Tegucigalpa as we had been. For some unexplained reason, his Tan Sahsa 727 jet plowed right into that mountainside just south of the city. His family waited two weeks for the positive identification and return of his body. He died on the same mountainside where I had, a couple of years earlier, envisioned our own team going down.

Charles's death underscored the seriousness of what we were doing. These trips are not all fun and games. They are sometimes serious, and sometimes they involve life and death. Charles invested his life in them.

So, why don't we just play it safe and stay home? Because God doesn't call us to play it safe. He calls us to go out on a limb and risk something for Him. He calls us to "The Great Adventure." A lot has happened on these trips and in our lives in the past 12 years. I can't tell you everything that's happened, but I can share a few of the highlights with you. I think you'll enjoy what you read. I hope you're challenged. Each story represents a different way students respond to God's working in their lives. It's hard to narrow the focus down to a few stories, and each story could be repeated literally dozens of times by students on Nazarene campuses across the United States and Canada. As you read the following stories, put yourself in the team members' shoes and relive the challenge with them. Who knows, maybe you'll find yourself on one of these adventures someday. It could happen. Fasten your seat belt!

Chapter 2

From Smallville to the Jungle

A SOPHOMORE RELIGION MAJOR from Tecumseh, Nebraska, Jon Kroeze, wanted to go on that first trip to Honduras mostly for the thrill of a new experience. It would be his first opportunity to get out of the country and see another part of the world. Several of his friends applied to go on the trip, so it seemed like a fun thing to do with them. He also saw it as a chance to involve himself in missions work as a testimony of his love for Christ.

The youngest of nine children, Jon grew up on a farm with four brothers and four sisters. His parents walked with God and provided their children with a rich spiritual heritage and example of Christlikeness. Growing up in that atmosphere made it easy for Jon to understand spiritual matters at the tender age of 6. "My mom talked with me one evening about spiritual things and what it meant to be a follower of Jesus. My spiritual taste buds were prepared, so in our living room that evening, we knelt together beside the couch, and in a simple way I asked Jesus to come into my heart." Jon began his personal relationship with Christ in that moment.

As Jon grew, he began to think about the future. He asked his mother a very mature question at age 11. "We were riding along on Highway 50 about 15 miles north of Tecumseh, Nebraska, when I asked, 'What do you think I'll be when I grow up?'" Jon's mom responded, "Jon, that is not for me to tell you. But if you walk with God, He will show you what He wants you to be."

In the silent moments that followed, Jon sensed God directing his heart toward full-time ministry. The thought didn't thrill him since he already dreamed of becoming a commercial airline pilot. He didn't think much about his vocation in the years that followed, but that all changed at the age of 16 at Camp Maranatha. Dr. Jim Diehl spoke on full surrender to Christ. Jon decided right then and there, if God wanted him in the ministry, that's what he'd do. He surrendered his dreams for God's. He began listening for God's voice in a new way.

Jon came to MidAmerica to prepare himself for God's work. During his second year of college, he applied to go on our work trip. Preparation required a lot of effort: raising money, getting shots and a passport, and gathering all sorts of supplies for the work site. As he did all of this, Jon remarked to a friend, "I'm sure glad God hasn't called me to be a missionary, because I wouldn't want to go through all of this inconvenience as a way of life."

Before he knew it, the preparation ended and Jon found himself working in the hot sun of Honduras. After his first few days on the mission field, he looked forward to going home soon and adding some new pictures to his scrapbook. Like many of us, Jon enjoyed the benefits and privileges of an American heritage. He always had food on his table and clothes on his body. He even had spending money for a few of the extras of life. He enjoyed friends and family in a protected rural environment. This "Honduras thing" was a big change for him. The big city, the terrible poverty, the strange sights and sounds, the weird foods, and the unique customs overwhelmed him. His world had been enlarged, and he wasn't sure he was ready for that. Jon anxiously anticipated using the return portion of his airline ticket to return to his comfort zone.

Somewhere in the middle of the week, however, something stirred in Jon's heart. He sensed the intense satisfaction of giving his life away in service to some of the neediest people in the western hemisphere. He realized he was making an investment in their lives. He awakened to the fact that this was the real world. Two-thirds of the world live just as these people live—trying to find enough food to make it to tomorrow. He experienced for the first time in his life the absence of "necessities" like running water, indoor plumbing, electricity, ice, air conditioning, hot showers, cold drinking water, a private bedroom, a bed, variety in diet, and a host of other things. He noticed that the missionaries lived without many of these conveniences as well. He saw spiritual hunger all around him, and an openness to the gospel that he had not experienced at home. He worked side by side with missionaries and felt their heartbeat and passion for souls. He also saw the tremendous sense of fulfillment in their lives.

All of these thoughts and experiences came together for Jon on the last day of the trip. Our team sat in a circle as each member shared one thing that he or she learned that week. When Jon's turn came, he said something that etched a place in my memory forever. I can still hear his words ringing in my ears. "When I was getting ready for this trip, I was so glad God hadn't called me to be a missionary. I didn't want to be one. I still don't really feel called, but if God did call me, I would be willing."

Jon returned and finished his sophomore year of school. Life resumed a normal routine—sort of. He hadn't noticed it during the trip, but after he returned from Honduras, Jon's thinking started going in new directions. He went to the electronics store to buy a new stereo system for his room but left the store without it. He looked at the price tag and realized the stereo cost more than most of his friends in Honduras made in a year. He decided that the stereo he currently owned met his needs. He went to the mall to get some new clothes but left them on the rack. He walked out of the store without even trying them on. The clothes hanging in his closet still fit him and looked nice.

All of the price tags on the things in Jon's life started switching places. The trinkets of life like shiny new cars and fancy stereo systems dropped in value. His friends in Honduras had taught him to be satisfied just with the Lord. He didn't feel he needed to give all of his possessions away; he just needed to keep all of the material possessions in their proper place.

Jon got out pictures of those Honduran friends and started thinking about their commitment to God and how rich it made their lives. He began to view people through God's eyes. He started loving the people around him in a new way. He saw their physical and spiritual needs as he had never seen them before. Jon had rubbed shoulders with those same people before the trip, but he hadn't noticed them then. Now he did, and he wanted to help them.

Jon began to learn that the Christian life is much like breathing; he took in the blessings of the Lord, and he needed to give them out to others. He had to exhale before he could inhale again. His Christian journey took on new depth as he involved himself in ministry. So Jon got involved in selfless service to people around him. He volunteered at the local rescue mission and gave extra effort to school friends in need. As he did this, he entered into a whole new realm of spiritual development, and he couldn't go back to his former world.

Jon's parents raised him to seek God and do His will, and he had attempted to do that. He thought he had the world and his place in it all figured out until now. His small-town view of life wasn't big enough to hold his new experiences.

The Honduran culture, with its unfamiliar sights, sounds, and smells, the funny looking bugs crawling all over everything, the roosters that crow all night, and the absence of his favorite CDs and television programs had overwhelmed him at first. But now, back home, everything came together and blew Jon's small-town view of life apart. It wasn't that he had been wrong before; he'd just been thinking too small. As he read his Bible and prayed, a whole new view of life began to form—a bigger picture with God calling him into this new world to do more than he had ever dreamed before. He had planned to pastor or evangelize. Now, he felt confused. He wasn't so sure about that anymore. He did know one thing for sure, though. He couldn't sit around and do nothing. He needed to get involved and do something.

These thoughts and feelings, like seeds, had been planted in his heart and mind in Honduras. Now they were starting to sprout. He began thinking about cross-cultural missions. All of these seeds grew throughout his junior year of college. Jon slowly began to feel that God might be leading him into missions work as a career.

The work trip to Honduras only lasted one week, but it still impacted his life more than a year later. He couldn't get away from it. His friends from Honduras kept visiting his imagination, calling him to think globally. That trip kept turning his world upside down. He hadn't realized it at the time, but it became a defining moment in his life, a focal point for all that would come afterward. His language, his actions, his purchases, and his plans—all filtered their way through his Honduras experience.

Jon Kroeze stands in front of the newly constructed parsonage in Honduras.

Jon didn't know if God wanted him to be a missionary, but he wanted to know for sure. So he made arrangements through International Headquarters and spent the following summer working as a volunteer in Swaziland, Africa—just to see if God might confirm his feelings. Jon relates, "I remember clearly God spoke to my heart in Africa and said, 'You said you would be willing to be a missionary should I call. Are you still willing?'" Jon responded, "Yes, Lord." He returned from Africa with the certainty that his call to full-time Christian service involved the mission field. He was so excited to tell me the good news that he called me from a pay phone late one night as soon as his plane landed back in Chicago.

Jon began to shift gears in his life as soon as he

got back to the United States. He sat down and assessed his situation in life. He hadn't picked a specific career yet. He did not have a wife or children to think about. He didn't own a house or an expensive car. He didn't have a lot of debt or any binding obligations in his life. He could freely follow wherever God led without any hindrances or delays. And that's exactly what he did.

Jon finished his bachelor's degree at Mid-America, then took missions courses at Nazarene Theological Seminary. He met Mary-Lou while at NTS and told her about his missionary call. She had a missionary call too. In time a bridge of love developed and they married. They pastored a church in Caledonia, Ontario, for seven years. During this period of time Jon and Mary-Lou were blessed with two children—Sarah and Jonathan.

Then they spent a year in Quebec learning the French language. All of this preparation took place across 10 years following the Honduras trip. Finally, his family received their missionary appointment to Rwanda, Africa, and they departed for that area on September 19, 1997.

Jon summarizes his philosophy of ministry by saying, "We all like to invest in something. We all like to be successful at something. If we're going to invest in something that lasts, I believe we must invest in people's lives. We must point them to Christ; this is an investment not only for a lifetime but for eternity."

Chapter 3

A Compass Without a Needle

AN "UNDECLARED" FRESHMAN—that's how we categorized Jon North when he arrived on our campus. Some students come to college with a plan. They know what major they want to study and what they want to do with their lives once they graduate from college. Most don't, however, and only half of the freshman class each year at our university even declares a course of study when they arrive. So at least in this respect Jon was a typical freshman.

Jon grew up in a Christian home in the Kansas City area with two brothers. His older brother, Rob, served as student body president at Olivet Nazarene University. Jon wanted to venture out on his own and not be known as Rob's little brother, so he decided to attend MidAmerica Nazarene University instead. He didn't go very far from home the day he moved his stuff into the dorm, but he was far enough away to be out from under the eye and influence of his parents.

Jon's commitment to Christ lacked depth when he arrived on campus, and he felt more freedom than he had ever known in his life. There was no one to wake him up in the morning or tell him to go to bed at night; no one to make him go to class or ask him what he was doing with his time. A shallow commitment to Christ and an abundance of free choice were a dangerous combination. Jon explored his newfound freedom that freshman year and broke a few school rules in the process. He was not a wicked or violent person—but not exactly a model student either.

Once the school year got under way, Jon's life began heading in a dangerous direction away from the Christian path. Many times Jon wandered into my Bible class and sat with his best friend in the very last row. He was present in body only; his mind was a thousand miles from studying the Bible. Socializing in the dorm and having a good time with his football buddies topped his list of priorities. He wasn't learning much, but he sure was having a lot of fun.

That attitude continued throughout Jon's freshman year. He appeared disconnected from the flow of campus life, but a lot of thoughts ran through his head. He kept asking himself, "What are you going to do with your life? What matters to you, anyway?" And he kept coming up with the same haunting answer: "I don't know." He had it all—good friends, a car, good health, and an envied position on the football team. But all of it meant nothing. Without a guiding purpose, he was heading nowhere fast. His life resembled a compass without a needle.

Jon's life bankrupted at the end of his freshman year as he returned home from college. He hit bottom in every area. He didn't go to church any more than he had to. He didn't have a relationship with God. His freshman year grades weren't good, and he had absolutely no idea what he wanted to do with his life. He had no self-confidence, little self-esteem, and didn't think his life could amount to anything significant. He left school defeated and wandering. Jon was smart, personable, and a very likable guy, but without a vision for his future, he drifted on the sea of indecision like a ship without a sail.

Jon started thinking about his messed-up life one July evening about bedtime. The picture looked pretty dark. Then it happened. Like the prodigal son in Jesus' parable, Jon came to himself. A light switched on in his head. He realized that his lack of focus and his sense of despair began with his spiritual bankruptcy. Right then and there, Jon decided to commit his life fully to Christ. Nothing else seemed to work for him. He'd been raised in a Christian home, so he knew the way back. Why not give Christ a try with this mess he found himself in? It couldn't hurt.

With Christ now at the center of his life, Jon's perspective on everything began almost immediately to change for the better. He came by my office a few weeks later and talked with me about his decision to follow Christ. Jon is not an emotional guy, so he didn't laugh or cry as he told me his story. But I knew that his decision had affected him in a profound way. He didn't look any different, but the change in his outlook shone through his conversation. His coolness toward God and spiritual matters had vanished. He had a new resolve to find direction for his life.

Some of Jon's professors had believed in him even when he hadn't believed in himself; he had a lot of untapped potential. Now he had the will to become all that God had in mind for him. Neither he nor I knew at the time what that might be. But one thing we knew: Jon remained open to whatever God wanted to do with him.

I happened to be working on plans for our next work trip the day Jon stopped by my office. Airline schedules, notes from Headquarters, and project proposals lay scattered across my desk. I encouraged him to apply to go on the trip. I didn't know if he would be interested in that kind of a challenge—hard construction work in the hot sun in a third world country with a lot of inconvenience—but I knew he would be great at it. His strong athletic build and his thrilling Christian witness would be welcome assets to our team. In God's providence, he did apply to go to Georgetown, Guyana.

Guyana proved to be a hard trip. Our late night layover in Port of Spain, Trinidad, left us only four hours to sleep before we traveled on to Georgetown. Guyana is a socialist country, so government officials searched every inch of our luggage when we entered the country. We also knew they were watching our activity throughout the week. Food was scarce, so we brought almost everything we ate with us. The people of Guyana survived on fish and fruit.

At that time, the economy of Guyana was a mess. Inflation had spiraled out of control, and the currency devalued three times in the week we were there. The necessities of life were hard to come by; we even had trouble getting bottled gas to cook our food. Construction supplies proved hard to find too. Even after we found them, store clerks often refused to sell them to us. They didn't want their supplies wasted on a church building. Cows grazed in the yard of the house where we stayed, bringing flies and fresh fertilizer with them. Roaches as big as mice swarmed our work site. We slept under mosquito nets at night to keep the thousands of swarming little vampires off us. One time it rained nonstop for 31 hours. The sewer ditch in front of our house overflowed and ran a foot deep throughout the house. Live fish and sewage flowed freely under our beds. Our entire team spent two days together on the second floor of the house. Messy cleanup followed once the water receded.

Jon was right in the middle of all this and loved every minute of it. Every minute except bedtime, that is. Jon started waking up every morning with what we thought was a rash. Then as his problem worsened nightly, we discovered small holes in the wood of his bed. Bugs apparently burrowed into the wood and came out each night to bite Jon as he slept. Add to that the fact that he rolled against his mosquito netting in his sleep one night and mosquito bites covered his back the next morning.

He didn't seem to mind, however. He just worked all the harder and figured it as part of his sacrifice for the work of Christ.

Jon fell in love with the work and with the local people. He was especially impressed with our national hosts, Rev. and Mrs. Robert Dabydeen. Our entire team learned a vital lesson from the Dabydeens about maintaining a Christlike spirit and going forward with the work of the Lord in the midst of extreme political oppression. Rev. Dabydeen taught us how to conduct ourselves to avoid conflict with the government. We learned the things we could do and not do in public. If we did not guard our behavior, *he* could be arrested for failure to properly chaperon us. We soon learned that he and his family lived with constant frustration as a way of life. Yet they never complained about their difficult situation, and they displayed a wonderful sense of humor and love for Christian service.

Daily life in Guyana involves standing in long lines to get one or two food items, searching all over town for supplies, and a host of other tasks too numerous to mention. We realized that hosting work teams posed added difficulties to the Dabydeens' lives. However, they willingly served in order to see the work of the Lord move forward. Rev. and Mrs. Dabydeen spent their entire week searching for supplies, tools, and fresh fruit for our team. Both maintained cheerful smiles and pleasant spirits no matter how frustrating the circumstances became. Jon was deeply moved by their strong commitment to do God's work in this difficult location.

It made his frustration with bug bites and over-flowing sewers seem pretty small.

Everything about that Guyana trip impacted Jon: the work, the play, the worship services, the fun times, the wonderful Spirit-filled Christians, and the needs of the people with whom we worked. Like puzzle pieces, they all fit together to form a new picture of life for Jon. No sooner had we returned from Guyana than Jon started talking about wanting to go on our next work trip, wherever that might be.

The next school year brought the tragedy of Charles Morrow's plane crash. Our entire campus grieved his loss. We wanted to do something to honor his memory and pay a tribute to his dedication to Christ. We decided to participate with the other Nazarene colleges and universities in constructing a church building for Charles in Costa Rica. Jon was the first to sign up for the project.

The work in Costa Rica was hard, but living conditions were not as difficult as in Guyana. Because Charles Morrow was a member of our extended family, we wanted to build the bulk of the church building ourselves. Jon led the way in pushing our team to work harder and longer hours than we planned to work. By the end of the week, the four walls of the church were up and ready for the roof. The local Christians were so excited to see their new building take shape that they scheduled a service following our last work day. We worshiped together before returning home. We ended our week with a lot of tears, hugs, and sad good-byes.

Congregation at Charles Morrow Memorial Church in Liberia, Costa Rica.

God brought several wonderful Christians into Jon's life that week in Costa Rica, just as He had done in Guyana. None made a bigger impression than Mr. Vesente Guadamuz. He was a soft spoken, unassuming, mostly gray-haired man who endeared himself to all of us. Mr. V., as we affectionately called him, was our construction foreman, but he was much, much more. We soon realized we were in the presence of a great saint of God; his life had an unmistakably special quality about it. You did not have to talk with Mr. V. very long to know how much he loved his Lord and the Church, what a burden he carried for the lost, and how deeply he longed for the extension of the Church of Jesus Christ. His concern was always for others: for the two widows with their families who needed a new house and for the congregation in this Costa Rican town of Liberia who needed a new church building.

Mr. V. worked all day at our construction site, then slept at the work site with the tools at night. We offered him a bed at our residence, but he refused. The tools were too expensive and hard to replace to run the risk of being stolen. I cried the first time I walked in the toolshed and saw the way he was living in order to build this new church. I made sure all of the students saw it as well. This was the best illustration of sacrifice for service they would ever see in their lives: a little mat on the ground, a comb, a cup, a razor, soap, a towel, a small bag with a few clothes in it, and that's all. After seeing that toolshed, we all made fresh commitments to God, expressing our willingness to sacrifice for His work.

We learned that Mr. V. was from San Jorge, Rivas, Nicaragua, where the Church of the Nazarene began in that country over 53 years ago. He knew the early missionaries personally and worked closely with them. He was responsible for constructing church buildings all over Nicaragua and for crafting the pulpits, altars, and pews for them. Even today people talk about his handiwork over the years. The war in his homeland forced him to move his family to Costa Rica, where he continued to build churches for the glory of God. He missed Nicaragua but was not bitter about having to move. He just quietly worked for the Lord in his new home.

Missionary Duane Rensberry related to us that one evening after work, Mr. V. unburdened his heart about his desire to see the church become more effective in winning the lost. They prayed together for God's blessing, guidance, and direction. He sacrificed his whole life for that burden. Jon North worked with Mr. V. in Costa Rica, and he would never be the same after that week.

Guyana and Costa Rica worked together to revolutionize Jon's view of life and his commitment to Christ, and by the end of the Guyana trip, a lot of thoughts worked their way into Jon's mind. He enjoyed the privilege of growing up in the warm cocoon of a Christian home with Christian parents and a caring Christian community at his home church. Food, clothing, and shelter were readily available to him. He attended a Christian university near his home, where he made many strong Christian friendships. He worked a job at a local furniture store delivering furniture to customers every afternoon following football practice. He called home any time he needed to talk with his parents. And he had a girlfriend, one of the nicest young ladies on campus.

Nevertheless, these thoughts from the Guyana and Costa Rica trips kept haunting him. There was such a big, needy world outside of Kansas City—so many people with so much hurt and so few resources. He recalls those days with, "I returned from that first trip with a newfound sensitivity for the needs of others and a true heart of compassion for them. God continually spoke to me on that trip about my responsibility to meet the needs of others. Up to that week, I'd been thinking, 'What's the use? There are so many needs. I can't even make a dent.' But when I stood back and looked at the big picture, I could see the part each person played in meeting needs—one at a time."

From that point on, the light began to dawn in Jon's thinking: one person or one group of students *can* make a difference in this world. After his first week on the mission field, his team left behind a remodeled Christian school, medical clinic, and district center. After his second trip, a beautiful church stood in Liberia, Costa Rica, on what had been a vacant lot just a week earlier. Both teams had made friends and touched lives.

With that new insight, self-confidence grew in Jon. His indecision about life's purpose gave way to action. He began looking for opportunities to make a difference in people's lives. He quickly surfaced as a spiritual leader and an example on the university football team. He volunteered his time in ministry projects around campus. Ministry took on a whole new definition for him. He didn't sense a call to preach, but he sure felt called to active ministry. The work trips left Jon a different young man.

It didn't happen overnight, but God used Jon's mission experiences to plant and develop a vision in his heart for a vocational call. One afternoon toward the end of his senior year Jon stopped by my office. He felt a little stressed; graduation day was just around the corner. He didn't know what he wanted to do after he graduated from college, but he wanted to be involved in compassionate ministry of some sort. Jon told me, "I want to spend the rest of my life continuing the type of work we did on the work trips, but I don't think I'm supposed to be an ordained minister."

I had no idea what Jon could do with that vision. I prayed with him that God would open the door for him to use his gifts and abilities in this area that burdened him.

One of the best things that happened in Jon's life during college was his girlfriend, Faith Palmer. She helped him grow in a variety of ways and mature into a responsible adult. Jon had such positive experiences on his work trips that he wanted Faith to go on one. So she went on our team to Mexico. She, too, developed a heart for ministry that helped her in her nursing career. But she couldn't tell Jon what to do with his life any more than I could.

Jon graduated from MidAmerica with a degree in international agrimissions and went on to get his masters of business administration degree from MNU. He and Faith married during that period of time. While he studied for his masters, he worked across the street from our campus at a humanitarian organization called Heart to Heart International, which gave him an opportunity to use his business degree and minister to human need at the same time.

The mission of Heart to Heart International is to locate thousands of tons of donated medical supplies and humanitarian relief and to airlift them to troubled spots of our world. They respond to both catastrophic disasters like earthquakes or hurricanes and to long-term plights like famine and overpopulation. Jon hired on just as the organization began, and he has grown with the organization. Currently he is the director of administration and finance for this global outreach. In this capacity, Jon takes supplies into places where the church is not yet welcome and brings aid to hurting humanity. He is a world Christian; his territory of responsibility spans the globe. One flight went to Russia, another to Vietnam, one to North Korea, another to India. A recent trip took him to China.

Jon's efforts literally impact hundreds of thousands of lives worldwide. I never would have dreamed such a big dream for Jon, but God did. Jon followed his heart, and God led him into this exciting ministry. He's not a missionary or an ordained minister, but he surely is in ministry. God took his commitment and willing heart and placed him in a strategic location for doing His work. God has a way of doing that—of matching our talents and abilities with professions or tasks that help us fulfill His direction for our lives.

Jon also actively participates in his local church by teaching a college Sunday School class. He's helping college students find direction for their lives just as he found it for his at that stage of life. He involves them in lay ministry, showing them the incredible fulfillment it brings to life. He summarizes the impact of the work trips on his life by saying, "They helped me realize what God will do when we are willing to do what He asks and trust Him for the outcome."

Chapter 4

Cat Guarding the Parakeets

HE COULD HAVE WALKED right off the set of some inner-city cop show. Only this guy wasn't a Hollywood actor. He was flesh and blood for real and mean to the bone. Some pretty tough characters control the mean streets of the inner city. But none of them was tougher or more street smart than Brian—stocky build, Marine-style haircut, tough as nails.

Raised by his mother in a gang-infested neighborhood of Denver, Colorado, Brian Watson grew up on the hard side of life. His mother did her best to save him from the destructive influences of his surroundings, but he rebelled against everything she tried to teach him. He didn't fit in her world, and he knew it. He didn't want to fit. His home was the streets and his family the gangs. He'd rather be on the streets with his friends.

Every time Brian turned around he was in trouble—trouble with the law for vandalism and petty theft; trouble at school for getting into fights, skipping class, and mouthing off to teachers; trouble at home for being disrespectful and lying to his mother and for beating up his own brother and sister. If it was wrong, bad, dishonest, or disrespectful, Brian did it, and with little or no remorse for his actions. This wasn't just a teenage stage he passed through either. He stood toe-to-toe with authority figures from the time he was old enough for his mouth to get him in trouble. He never took anything off of anyone.

That's how Brian lived through elementary school, junior high, and senior high school. He did it all, and he had the time of his life, living it up on the wild side. Brian was having fun with no intention of stopping.

As is true for so many who lose their way, Brian's mother prayed for him daily and took him to church with her for as long as she could get him to go. She attended Denver First Church of the Nazarene. Even though he chose to walk down the wrong side of the road of life, somewhere in the distant shadows of his past lingered a faint memory of the right way. Perhaps that is the reason for his startling announcement one hot summer day following his senior year of high school.

Brian hadn't taken his studies seriously so it took him five and a half years to graduate from high school. He realized he needed more education than he had. He wanted to get away from home, his mom, and his haunting past. Maybe a new start would be good for him. He dreamed of playing football in college. So that hot day in July he announced to his family, "I am going to attend Mid-America Nazarene University!"

Unbelievable! Why on earth would a street punk like Brian want to attend MidAmerica? Who knows! Nobody believed he would follow through on this outlandish plan, but he did. He packed up a few of his things and moved to Olathe, Kansas. It didn't take long for him to realize he had made the biggest mistake of his life. His non-Christian, pleasure-seeking, self-centered lifestyle blended into the Christian university environment like oil on water. Brian got busted for violating just about every rule the school had. He wasn't ready to make a complete break with his past, and the university wasn't ready to let him break its rules.

Brian's misery level at MidAmerica hit an all-time high. He completed his first year of college, then vowed never to return as he moved his things back to Denver. He didn't move back in with his mother upon his return, however. He got an apartment of his own near his friends in downtown Denver. It wasn't much, but it was a place he could call his own. That apartment represented the direction his life headed—farther away from his Christian heritage.

Being on his own didn't go so well for Brian. The days ahead brought him more uncertainty and darkness than he'd anticipated. He recalls, "The following year was the absolute worst year of my life. I came to the point where I turned my back completely on God and everything that had to do with Him. I decided to live totally for myself and do what I wanted to do, no matter what the cost." People say he turned uglier and darker than he had ever been before he went to college.

One day while Brian was sitting in an old, worn swivel chair in his downtown Denver apartment, his life bottomed out. He remembers, "I felt so hopeless, helpless, and lifeless. I was so empty and so low." Just then the phone rang. It was his mother calling to check on him. She'd invited him to attend church with her a hundred times before and had him throw the invitation back in her face, but she kept inviting.

She called to see if he would go to church with her the following morning for the special Father's Day service. He didn't care anything about going to her church, but he got tired of her bugging him about it. So, he reluctantly agreed to go with her just to get her off his back. He felt so badly about the way things were going in his life at that time that he figured what would it hurt to drop in on the church folks for old times' sake?

His motive for going was probably wrong, but God gripped Brian's heart in that service. Everything the pastor said spoke directly to him. He painted a picture of Brian's life in living color. The Holy Spirit of God moved him in a way he had never felt. Before the service ended, Brian found himself at the altar at the front of the church, giving his heart and life to God. He doesn't even remember how he got there. But he made a decision to follow God that morning—a decision that changed everything in his life from that day forward.

He had vowed a year earlier that he'd *never* go back to MidAmerica Nazarene University, but that's exactly where he headed in the fall. Word spread like a mountain fire around campus, "Get the kids in; watch your pockets. Brian Watson is back!" It sounds funny now, but it was true. I warned my 11-year-old son Brent, who hung around the campus after school, to stay away from "that Watson character." I remember the first time I saw him in the hallway of the religion building after he returned. The chip on his shoulder was replaced by a big smile. His face literally glowed with the presence of his newly found Lord. I didn't know this new guy; it wasn't the Brian who returned to Denver a year earlier.

Brian grew in his walk with God, and he began to sense God's leading to become a schoolteacher. So, he switched majors. It turned out that he was a natural with kids. Who would have guessed? This is the guy we had tried to keep our kids away from a year ago, and now he was working with elementary children! That's sort of like getting a cat to guard your parakeets.

The next year Brian applied to go on our work trip to the Dominican Republic. For some strange reason, I felt led to put him on our team. Still, I was unsure. He had come a long way all right, but was he ready for an international ministry trip? We were about to find out. The dean of students advised Sue and me to give him a chance.

I must admit, Brian threw himself into the work of laying concrete blocks to build a school for the children of Altos de Chavon, a community of 15,000 near Santo Domingo. He worked hard on the project with the rest of the team. By the end of

A wall goes up on the school in the Dominican Republic

the week, he was best friends with the local construction foreman. You'd have thought they were long-lost brothers to watch them work together.

The construction foreman was not the only one to affect Brian's life that week. Perhaps the most powerful impact by a national individual in the Dominican Republic came from a 10-year-old boy named Jason, who lived in a modest shack with a dirt floor and tin roof in the Haitian squatter village near our work site. Several of the students were making medical home visits with a missionary nurse one day when they met him. They took several more students back to his home the next day. His influence has been with us ever since.

Jason was in the last stages of terminal bone cancer. His right leg had been amputated, and his body was racked with pain. His young father had recently died of a broken heart from watching his son suffer. His mother was trying to care for his constant pain while she grieved over her husband's death. Our students changed his bandages, then gathered around his bed and sang songs, prayed, and performed an impromptu skit with sock puppets. They blew bubbles with a soap solution and let them pop around his little face. Jason was too weak to respond with anything more than a strained smile. His mother sobbed quietly in the background.

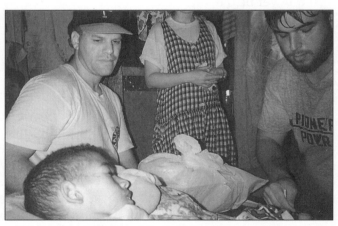

Brian Watson *(left)* and Fred Warkentine *(right)* minister to Jason in the Dominican Republic.

The only thing that made the situation easier was the assurance that Jason was ready to meet the Lord. His heart was filled with the Lord's presence and it showed. What a sight to see the team ministering to this precious child in such dire poverty and pain! The memory of that afternoon at Jason's bedside always brings deep emotion and tears to all of us who were there. We did not know it at the time, but one of our team members, Fred Warkentine, accepted God's call to become a medical missionary while sitting by Jason's side. Fred is studying in medical school right now. The missionaries wrote us the week after we left the Dominican Republic and told us that Jason had gone on to be with the Lord. The offering we left paid for his burial. Brian Watson would never be the same after visiting Jason's house.

Looking back over the Dominican Republic experience, Brian admits, "The last thing going through my mind was that the trip would be a life-changing moment for me. But it was. It was through that experience that I developed a deep heart's desire to be a missionary."

A missionary! Who would have predicted that a year before or even the week before? None of us! The trip had changed Brian's whole value system. Now he wanted to be a schoolteacher *on the mission field.* As soon as we returned from the Dominican Republic, Brian started talking about going on the next work trip to El Salvador. And he did too. He served as team captain of that group, which built a medical clinic next door to a Nazarene church near San Salvador.

Brian and the pastor of the church established a strong friendship during their week of working together. They talked, joked, and arm wrestled throughout the week as they worked on the building. In the midst of it all, the pastor talked to Brian about his vision of winning the lost of his neighborhood to Christ and of helping the children of the area. Brian's heart was touched by the pastor's heart and the hurting people all around him. He felt a deep, inner tug to stay and work in that location. But he had to return to school. He left El Salvador more determined than ever that he would be back to serve on the field someday.

Brian applied to go on the work trip to Venezuela his senior year in college. We didn't know what they were, but we felt God had other plans for Brian. He graciously accepted our decision not to take him to Venezuela, though it hurt his feelings a bit. He wasn't sure what God wanted to do with his life once he graduated, but he still believed it involved elementary school and missions. A few weeks after we announced the Venezuela team without Brian's name on it, God brought all of the pieces of the puzzle together for Brian in a very unusual way.

His home church in Denver was preparing to send a Work and Witness team to build a school building in Benque Viejo, Belize, in Central America. Someone in the church offered to pay Brian's way if his professors would allow him to miss a few extra days of class. Everyone agreed Brian should go.

The Denver team arrived in Belize, but Brian never made it to the work site. One of the classrooms filled with children had no teacher. When the school principal discovered that Brian had already student-taught and was ready for a classroom, he offered it to him. For two weeks Brian had the time of his life. He knew this was it—God's plan for him. God spoke to Brian's heart on that trip. "I need you here in Belize. Will you come?" "Yes, Lord, I'll come," Brian answered.

At the end of the two-week trip, Brian promised his classroom of children that he would return to them. When he got back to the United States, he finished his last few weeks of the spring semester and graduated with a degree in elementary education. In the meantime, he contacted Nazarene Headquarters with his dream to return to Belize. With God's guidance, all of the paperwork quickly fell into place, and Brian was on his way back to Howard Smith Nazarene School. Brian's last letter to me is a fitting testimony of his life: "I am a living testament of God's amazing grace and love. God has called me! He has called me to be a child of His! He has called me to develop a deeper relationship with Him. And Belize is the place where I am developing that calling. Once again, God has proven that He can take an ordinary, simple man and use him to touch the world. To God be all the glory!"

At this writing, Sue and I have just returned from our 1997 C.A.U.S.E. trip to Belize. Our work team spent the week working with Brian. We visited his school and met his classroom full of children. It's obvious that he loves his students, and they love their teacher. A special bond joins them. Words cannot describe how proud we were to see him living in the center of God's will and impacting young lives for the Lord.

Chapter 5

He with the Most Toys Wins

LARRY WEST HAD THE WORLD by the tail on a downhill pull. He enjoyed the privilege of growing up in a Christian home. Both of his parents worked, so his family enjoyed a fairly comfortable lifestyle. All of his physical needs were met and so were most of his wants. Larry liked that lifestyle, but he wasn't satisfied with the level of comfort his parents afforded him. He wanted *more*—bigger and better of everything. So, he finished high school with a life goal to make more money than his parents had made and achieve an even higher standard of living than he had previously enjoyed. And he hid this ambition behind a Christian mask.

His heart ached for something. He wasn't sure what it was. Maybe a wife? "Yeah, that's it," Larry thought, "I need a wife." He met a girl named Phyllis at Nazarene Youth Congress the summer before he left for college. They dated during his freshman year of college and married at the conclusion of the school year. That entire year his mind never focused on his college classes. He was too busy thinking about Phyllis. He only wanted to work and spend all his extra time with Phyllis. His grades reflected his priorities. In fact, he failed his Christian beliefs class three times, and that wasn't the only class he failed. After three years of attending college, Larry's transcript overflowed with Fs. He landed himself on academic probation, and the dean forbade him to take any new classes until he raised all of his Fs to at least Cs. But he didn't care; he had all he wanted in life—a good job and a young, pretty bride.

Larry thought he had it all. In his mind the formula was clear: good job + house + new car + pretty wife = success. Successful people are happy, Larry thought, simple as one-two-three. The formula may look good in television movies, but it didn't work in Larry's life. He was far from happy. Even though he was the envy of most of his friends, he was bored and had no satisfaction in life.

Larry decided the problem must be his job, so he got a better job that paid more money. Surely more money would make him happier. But he still had no satisfaction. Maybe his problem was his car; he traded his Ford in on a new Chevrolet—still no satisfaction. So, he decided his problem must be Phyllis. Larry decided that he needed a new wife. He told Phyllis plain and simple that he wanted a divorce. He also decided her Christianity was tying him down and he didn't need religion anymore. She was crushed by his rejection of her but continued to pray for Larry in silence. And through it all, Larry continued to wear his Christian mask.

A few weeks following his request for a divorce, Phyllis begged Larry to attend the revival with her at the local Church of the Nazarene. Larry wanted no part of it and made plans to be out of town the entire weekend. His plans fell through, however, and before he knew it, he found himself eating dinner at the pastor's house prior to the Thursday evening revival service.

Larry had fooled everyone with his Christian mask except Phyllis and his pastor, and they weren't going to give up on him. Following the meal, the pastor talked Larry into attending the church service. He was there in body only; his mind wandered a million miles away. He had decided he was too smart for this Christian stuff. He was strong and didn't need a "Jesus crutch" to lean on. He knew the trap the pastor had set for him by inviting him to church, and he wasn't going to fall for it.

But the Holy Spirit gripped Larry's heart during that revival service. He found himself mysteriously drawn back to church night after night, like a moth to the light. Finally, he surrendered to the power of God and gave his life to Christ. Things changed that night for Larry. "What a difference Jesus brought into my life," Larry remembers. "He showed me what a good wife I had, and I fell in love with her for real this time." In the following years God blessed their home with three children: Allen, Nancy, and Kay. Larry loved the Lord and his family, but his priorities in life still focused on making lots of money and buying as many material possessions as he could afford.

On his 30th birthday, Larry inventoried his life and decided his course was set for the rest of his productive adult years. Then God rocked his comfortable world one day as he read his Bible. He sensed God directing him toward full-time Christian service. How could God ask him to quit his job, sell his house, uproot his family, and go back to college to prepare for the ministry? After all, the die of his life was cast, and he had been a miserable failure at college besides. But God asked exactly that. After a tough year of wrestling with God, Larry finally found peace with his decision to enter MidAmerica once more, this time as a religion major.

That's when I met Larry. I was his faculty adviser. He filled me in on all the details of his life up to that point. I saw his former transcript littered with Fs, but I also saw tremendous potential in this young man with a new vision of God's call on his life.

Soon after Larry returned to college, he read about our first work trip to Belize in 1988 in the chapel bulletin. He didn't know why, but he sensed God wanted him to apply to go. It seemed like such a crazy idea. He and Phyllis had a family to support and a school bill to pay. They couldn't really afford it, but Phyllis agreed that Larry needed to go on this trip. He was accepted as a member of the Belize team and attended all of the preparation meetings. We talked about the potholes in the road, the bugs in bed, the mosquitoes swarming the sleeping net, the bus breaking down, and the poverty-stricken children. He was ready for anything this trip might throw at him.

But Larry wasn't ready for the first question someone asked him as soon as he arrived in Belize. A local church leader asked, "Would you be willing to stay and help us with our ministry here?" What a dumb question. Of course he couldn't stay. He had a wife, three children, and another year of school back in the States. "Stay?" Out of the question. He just came down here to help out for a few days.

District Superintendent Rev. Onesimo Pot met us at the Belize City airport that Friday afternoon. We fell in love with him before we pulled away from the airport. That first evening, Mrs. Pot served a generous meal at the district parsonage while Rev. Pot told his life story of growing up as a village boy near Benque Viejo (where Brian Watson now teaches). He then shared his burden for the ministry to the people in the Toledo District of Belize. He set our hearts on fire with his vision of what he wanted to see God do in the southern villages where we were going to work.

Bright and early the next morning we traveled 10 hours south on washboard, dirt roads to the village of Punta Gorda, a town on the Caribbean Sea at the southern tip of Belize. It was a beautiful trip through rain forests, over wooden bridges without side rails, and into dense jungles.

Once we settled down in Punta Gorda, we slept in the church sanctuary on pews under mosquito nets and ate rice and beans. We worked all day in the hot, humid air to build a dormitory for pastors' children from the mountains so they could attend school. Conditions were basic, but our team had a great time together.

Our group was scheduled to hold several evening services in the mountain village of San José. Like all of the mountain villages of Belize, San José had no electricity, no running water, no telephone service, and no source of public transportation. Mechanical problems with our old bus kept the team from going more than one night. I asked Larry and another team member, Beth Adams, to ride a moped to San José and represent our team at one of those services. Larry was the oldest member of our team, and Beth had experienced similar missions assignments. They were to conduct the church service, spend the night with the pastor, and ride down from the mountain the next morning. The plan sounded simple enough.

Larry and Beth were honored guests for dinner in the pastor's home. His home consisted of sticks driven into the ground for walls, with banana leaves for a roof and polished dirt for a floor. The food was cooked over an open fire at one end of the hut and served on a coffee table large enough for the two guests. And what did they have for dinner? Rice and beans. They almost always eat rice and beans for dinner in Belize.[2]

For two hours following dinner, the pastor's brother asked Larry questions about the Bible and faith. He absorbed the answers like a dry sponge. He showed Larry the only book he owned—a book given to him by a cult member. The cults had been attempting to persuade Christians belonging to churches throughout the mountain villages to join their groups. Their plan involved disrupting established churches rather than trying to win converts from the unchurched. Local churches suffered because of their efforts.

After the evening service, Larry talked with the pastor for a long time about cult activity in the area. The pastor lamented, "Missionaries come bringing Christ to us, and we believe and are saved. But then as the missionaries go, the wolves come. We do not know how to stop them, how to teach our people what is right. We need training."

Eventually, they blew out the kerosene lamp and went to bed, and Larry spent the longest night of his life. This was his first attempt at sleeping in a hammock, and every movement nearly tossed him overboard. He tried to lay perfectly still. The chicken under his hammock kept scratching for corn on the dirt floor. The cool mountain air blew through the slots between the stick walls. The roosters directly outside his hut made noise throughout the night. But those weren't the real reasons Larry couldn't sleep. Every time he nearly dozed off, he heard the words of the pastor ringing again in his ears, "We need training."

The next morning Larry and Beth rode the moped back down the mountain to Punta Gorda to rejoin our team. However, Larry couldn't get San José and the Nazarene pastor out of his troubled heart. That visit had begun a dramatic struggle in Larry's thinking.

The week of work on the dormitory soon ended. We headed back to the United States, but Larry still couldn't get his night in San José out of his troubled heart. The San José pastor's words kept playing in his head; over and over, back and forth they played. "We need training." Larry sat at the now familiar McDonald's during our New Orleans layover and thought about his materialistic model of success in life and his desire to accumulate money and things. He recalls that moment of truth, "It seemed almost un-American to be thinking such thoughts. I was a believer in the American dream: house, car, the whole nine yards. From my youngest days I accepted that what you had was the measure of your success. 'He with the most toys wins.' I now had seen a different life, and I could not go back to my days of innocence. I realized that success was not in a bankroll and other acquisitions but in relationships: my relationship with God, with my wife and family, and with other people. God had broken through my preoccupation with things and taught me a lesson I would never forget."

Upon arrival back home, Larry shared the highlights of his trip with Phyllis. He insisted that they needed to return to Belize—together this time. Charles Morrow, coordinator of the Belize project, made the arrangements; God provided the finances; and they returned to San José in two months. They conducted Vacation Bible School during the day and revival services in the evening. The children were responsive, and several adults even came to Christ.

Larry and Phyllis returned from their week of activity and agreed that they did not want any part of missionary service. They saw the sacrifices a missionary must make; they saw the scale of the work that needed to be accomplished; they felt the physical sickness and pain. They didn't understand exactly why God had wanted them to return to Belize that summer, but they knew it was not to give them a missionary call. They were ready to give all the money that needed to be given to missions, but they surely didn't want to live on the mission field. So they came back home and went back to work and their normal household routine of raising three children.

Three weeks following their Belize trip, the Wests attended the Kansas City District Nazarene World Mission Society Convention. Larry arrived late in the day, coming straight from work. The missionary had already spoken, and the business session was nearly concluded. While sitting at the very back of the sanctuary, he suddenly felt surrounded by God's presence. He was powerfully gripped by the love and peace of Christ. He heard no divine voice, yet he knew deep in his heart what God was saying to him. It was not a message but a mission. He recalls, "I knew He wanted me to become His missionary. In the back of College Church on a Wednesday afternoon, I was surprised by God. All I could do was say, 'Yes, Lord Jesus. Yes, I will go.'"

Larry went home that afternoon, but he didn't tell Phyllis about his encounter with God. How could he? They had just agreed they were not interested in becoming missionaries. Two weeks passed, and he could hold it in no longer. Finally one evening, he blurted out, "Phyllis, God has called me to be a missionary."

He expected her to cry and question his judgment. Instead, she quietly replied, "Oh, Larry, what took you so long? God called me to be a missionary two weeks ago in my devotional time." Both had accepted God's call in their hearts but hesitated to tell the other. Now they agreed upon God's new direction for their lives.

Larry and Phyllis participated in our work trip to Guyana during his senior year of college. It was a great confirmation to them of God's mission call on their lives. Larry finished his college career with honors, making straight A's his second time around. They pastored an area church for a few years and are now full-time missionaries in Indonesia. Today they are training pastors, fulfilling the vision God laid on Larry's heart that restless night in the hammock in San José, Belize.

I remember the pastor in San José frequently, and I strive to give my best to prepare my student pastors adequately for the ministry. The challenges of Indonesia are unique, and it is clear that I am also training future missionaries, young men and women who will leave their home island to go to another of Indonesia's many islands. They will enter another culture and learn another language, becoming channels of blessings to people of the same nation but of different tribes and customs.

Success is mine. I no longer own a home,

but I am at home in the love of Christ and in love with my neighbor. Yes, God still calls people like you and me to follow Him wherever He leads. It is the call to success. When you feel His leading for whatever plan He has for you, go with the assurance that God will go ahead of you, preparing the way. You will never be alone.

Larry and Phyllis have certainly proved that with their lives. They traded their toys for God's treasures.

* * * * *

Allow me to relate a personal experience from Belize, similar to Larry's San José experience. I did not know for several years about Larry's call to bring ministerial training to pastors like his friend in San José. However, the Lord was dealing with me about that same matter at the same time. My situation was, of course, a bit different from Larry's. He still needed more college training and pastoral experience to prepare him for his assignment. As a college professor of religion, I was immediately available to step right in to fill the need in Belize.

Our host pastor of the Punta Gorda church, Rev. Eldridge Brooks, expressed a deep hunger for more education, just as the San José pastor had begged Larry for further training. I told Rev. Brooks to discuss the matter with the other pastors on the district and the district superintendent. If they wanted it, I could come back and give them training in the ministerial course of study. Four months later I returned to Punta Gorda to teach.

I flew on a small plane directly into Punta Gorda from Belize City, and the flights from Kansas City took most of the day. Rev. Brooks met me at the small airstrip and took me directly to the church building. I couldn't believe my eyes when I stepped inside. There sat two rows of hungry pastors awaiting my arrival. I sat my bags down just inside the church door, took off my sunglasses, and wiped the sweat from my face, and before we introduced ourselves, one of the pastors asked, "How soon can we get started here?" My hopes of stretching out on a pew for a few minutes of rest from the long trip were tabled. These guys were too hungry to be kept waiting!

Within 10 minutes, we convened class. For nearly two weeks the pastors listened, took notes, and discussed the subject matter for 10 to 12 hours a day. I couldn't even get them to take a break! I figured they had to be as tired of listening as I was of talking. Not so. Finally after several days at this marathon pace, I asked, "Why don't you guys ever want to take a break?" Rev. Brooks quickly responded, "If you were as hungry to learn as we are, you wouldn't want to break either. We have waited for years for these classes." So we kept at it.

The pastors studied hard after class each evening. Electricity in Punta Gorda is limited. So one-third of the village blacks out each evening on a three-day rotation. On the nights we had no lights for studying, those faithful pastors read by candlelight or stood under nearby streetlights. I can still see them huddling around those streetlights, fighting bugs, and reading their assignments for the next day. It was thrilling to watch them devour their ministerial training like hungry children at mealtime.

For the next five summers I took a professor with me back to Belize for more pastor's classes. One of us taught until lunch, and the other until dinner. Then the pastors studied well into the night. Those men became my dearest friends in the world. Stories of our times together would fill a book. With time and a great deal of personal study, each one of them graduated from the ministerial course of study and received their ordination in the Church of the Nazarene. God met yet another need through our simple efforts.

Chapter 6

It Keeps Going
and Going and Going

SO FAR IN THIS BOOK we have talked about the life-changing influence of missions work for college students. We have also hinted that visible changes take place on the field—church buildings, Sunday School additions, parsonages, medical clinics, or schools are constructed or remodeled. Food, clothing, health, and hygiene supplies are distributed. Medical services are provided, and evangelism efforts are extended into the community.

However, some of the greatest results of our efforts happen on the field long after the teams return home. Sometimes the long-term results were planned as a part of the total strategy of a particular project. But more often than not, the good results that follow come under the leadership of the Holy Spirit, who takes the humble efforts of college students and blesses them far beyond their wildest hopes and dreams. God alone deserves the credit and praise for what He accomplishes. This chapter will highlight a few of the long-term results on the field.

* * * * *

Dr. Carlos Saenz was our field coordinator for the 1992 C.A.U.S.E. trip to Panama. He is a tall man both physically and spiritually. Compassionate, tenderhearted, and caring, he deeply impacted us. His story of commitment to the cause of Christ became a powerful example to us of a person who responded to God's call on his life.

While in medical school, Carlos served as a faithful layperson in his church. He wanted to increase his knowledge and understanding of the Scriptures, so he enrolled in some theology classes. When a pastor on the district retired, the district superintendent asked Carlos to serve as interim pastor of the Puente del Rey Church of the Nazarene in Panama City. God used this experience to call him to be a full-time pastor. Today his influence reaches beyond his local church. Dr. Carlos Saenz is the Nazarene Compassionate Ministries director for the Caribbean Region.

When we came to Panama, we quickly realized that this man could be earning a large salary as a medical doctor in Panama City. Yet he chose to live in a very modest home near his church and earn a modest salary as he fulfilled God's call on his life. We saw his infectious smile and sense of humor; we felt the love of Christ radiate from his heart; we knew he had the satisfaction in life that only comes from living in the center of God's will. We wanted to pattern our lives after his.

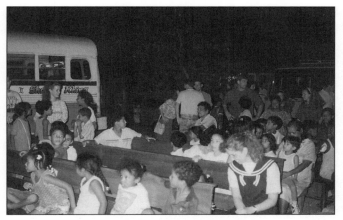
Children's crusade in Panama City

As the Panamanian Nazarenes hosted the C.A.U.S.E. teams, they began to see their country through the eyes of their visitors—and they didn't like all that they saw. Perhaps for the first time they noticed their hometown of Panama City filled with homeless children. They sensed God directing them to work with these street kids.

After our trips, Carlos conducted a two-year research of the problem. He sought effective ways to address it in Jesus' name. He first envisioned Nazarenes operating a drop-in house in an area where the problem was most serious. Then he got a better idea. Why not attack the problem at its source and develop a program to *prevent* children from becoming street kids?

So that's what he and his coworkers did. For two years, they trained staff members in psychological, emotional, social, and spiritual principles that would assist people in working through their differences and rebuilding families. They used the school that the Nazarene colleges built in the community of San Miguelito as their headquarters for operations. The principal of the school worked with government officials to get civic approval and support. In this way, their efforts were fully known to the government, and they gained needed credibility with people unfamiliar with the work of the Church of the Nazarene. At the time of this writing, 17 parents in the program have become new Christians, their families have been preserved, and their children are off the streets. Pray that God will continue to use this program to win more parents to himself and save more homes.

Another story of a long-term result spins off the previous one. Once these newly converted parents began to live out their Christian experience, they, too, received new eyes for their community. They saw the work done on their school and sewer system, and the cleanup efforts made by the college teams. They also saw the work that still needed to be done. With this new insight came a renewed initiative to continue the cleanup effort in their community. They are still working at the task, and they credit the Americans with getting them started. San Miguelito was once the slum of Panama City. Now the Church of the Nazarene has a strong presence in the community. Before the college students came, Nazarenes found it difficult to make an impact in this community. Now as a result of the family support program and the community restoration efforts, the Church of the Nazarene is at the center of community life there.

* * * * *

Betsabe Alvarez is from Caracas, Venezuela. Her story comes as an example of the types of things God has been doing with the young people of Venezuela. Betsabe is the sister of a Nazarene pastor in Caracas. She wanted to be involved in ministry but sought to give herself to something other than the compassionate ministry of her brother's church. Our college and university work teams came to Venezuela in 1995 at the height of her personal search for a ministry, and she decided to join in our efforts.

After we returned home, Betsabe sensed God leading her to start a prison ministry. The very idea scared her to death. How could a young Nazarene woman make an impact on hardened criminals? She tried to dismiss the idea from her thoughts but could not get away from it. God seemed to strengthen the impression that this was His call on her life. So she went to a prison in Caracas and witnessed to the men about her faith in Christ. To her amazement they responded, and some accepted Christ.

One of Betsabe's converts was a murderer named Luis. He had a bad reputation in Caracas and was one of the most feared men in prison. In time Luis was paroled and called into the ministry. He and Betsabe started a new church in Caracas; she is the pastor, and he is the evangelist for the church. What a story of God's power and grace to change lives and build His kingdom. We didn't plan for all this to happen, but God used our efforts. His plans are still being accomplished in Venezuela.

One reason for this might be that the Venezuela work project represented a new strategy for C.A.U.S.E. efforts on the mission field. Up to that time, teams pretty much came in, did their job, and left. They accomplished a lot of good, and great things happened with the local people after they returned home. Then, Gustavo Crocker, current director of Nazarene Compassionate Ministries, got an idea. What would happen if the youth from the field worked side by side with the teams when they came to minister? Venezuela was chosen as the test field because it was our newest work. The plan was to use the college students to jump-start compassionate ministry there.

So while the North American teams prepared to work in Venezuela, Venezuelan teens prepared not only to receive them but also to work alongside them. For the first time, we put as much effort into student preparation on the field as we did in the United States and Canada. For the first time, local Nazarene Youth International leaders were fully involved in the work on the field. For the first time, national youth attended an orientation camp to prepare them for their ministry. At this camp they learned about the vision and mission of Nazarene Compassionate Ministries and their role in it. We all envisioned future leaders emerging to continue the work long after the American teams returned home.

The cooperation of Americans and Venezuelans occurred as planned. Literally scores of Venezuelan high schoolers took off from school and left jobs to come and work alongside the Americans. The effort was always exciting and sometimes frustrating. It was exciting for us to watch the two groups of youth work, play, pray, sing, worship, and eat together. It was sometimes frustrating for our cooks, however, as numbers of hungry workers grew daily. On our project in Maracaibo, the cooks prepared for 35 people on the first day. By the end of the project, they were cooking for nearly 100. This same overwhelming success happened at each work site.

The Venezuelan students' lives were greatly impacted by the joint team effort. We were impressed with the quality of spiritual maturity of the team members who came and worked with us in Venezuela. Many of the people who had been on the fringe became actively involved! A large number of people were impacted in the communities where the combined teams worked. People came to evening services and gave their lives to God. Scores of "pumped-up" Christians in the churches no longer waited for the church to do the ministry but looked for ways to get involved. They also began taking a serious look at the needs around them and are still looking at how the Lord might be asking them to meet those needs.

We are learning of new developments in this

story all the time. God is still harvesting results from that effort. To date, 28 Venezuelan teens have accepted a call to full-time Christian service. Some of them are already in school preparing for their work. Venezuela now has a strong youth program with an emphasis on compassionate ministry. The national leadership was not content simply to receive the benefits of American teams; they wanted to join in the action. Thus, they organized their own work teams with 75 young people participating, and the work goes on.

*   *   *   *   *

Rev. Pedro Paulo F. Mattos was our field coordinator to Rio de Janeiro, Brazil, in 1996. What a powerhouse! He pastored his church of 1,200 people in the Nilopolis area of Rio; preached five to six times during the week; conducted four worship services on Sunday; looked after all the outreach ministries of the church, including their successful outreach to drug addicts; and coordinated the efforts of eight college and university teams. As if all that were not enough, Rev. Pedro Paulo also served as district superintendent!

We were most impressed with Pedro Paulo's friendly demeanor and genuine passion for souls. He embodied in his life all that Sue and I try to teach students about servant leadership. He did not just come out to our work site, stand under a shade tree, and watch us work in the hot Brazilian sun. He got right in line and passed bricks or moved concrete with us. He treated each of our team members as if he or she were the most important person in the world. He laughed and pranked like a teenager.

We also saw his leadership in the wonderful teen group from his church. Groups of young people on fire for the Lord do not just happen. They are cultivated by ministers with vision like Rev. Pedro Paulo. When our students worked with the Brazilian students for a couple of days, they commented on the powerful influence Rev. Paulo's ministry had on these teens. He challenged us all to be at our best for God and His work.

The situation in Brazil prior to the arrival of college work teams was different from that in earlier projects. Work teams had previously visited a country to get compassionate ministry started or continue a work just getting under way. Brazil was selected as the 1996 project site to celebrate the 10th anniversary of our mission efforts. This country was already doing as much with compassionate ministry as any field in South America. Leadership among both youth and adults was strong, and local involvement in compassionate ministry was high. The programming, leadership, motivation, enthusiasm, and vision were already in place. We wanted to know what would happen if teams came to lend a hand where things were already on fire.

As with the Venezuela project, the plan was to place a Brazilian young person to work alongside every North American team member. They, too, were given additional training in the mission of compassionate ministry. As with the Panama project, Brazilian leaders began to see their homeland with new eyes as they prepared for the arrival of visiting guests from the north.

The Brazilian leaders received holy boldness from the Lord as they dared to seek admission into one of the poorest and most tightly sealed slums in Rio de Janeiro: Morro Dona Marta. Dona Marta had a reputation. It was known as a headquarters for crime and a center for drug traffic in Rio. It was so controlled by the Red Command (a combination neighborhood watch and drug cartel) that Rio police dared not pass through its borders. When the police did try to make an occasional visit, Dona Marta transformed into a war zone.

Without a doubt, God worked a miracle as the Nazarene leaders negotiated with the Red Command. They agreed to allow Brazilian and American youth to come and lend them a hand in their community in Jesus' name. Other Christian groups in the Rio area looked on in amazement! Their requests to work in that particular slum had been denied. They did not understand how the Nazarenes got permission to enter Dona Marta. But we knew it was God's work.

For the Americans, the Dona Marta experience was a highlight of the trip. None of us will ever be the same after working there. But the greater and longer lasting results probably occurred in the lives of the Brazilian young people. They saw poverty and deprivation as they had never seen it before right in their own hometown. We had to leave after a short ministry opportunity, but they had the privilege of staying and continuing the work that we began together. Our combined efforts encouraged them to work harder for the Lord in their hometown. They're still at it today.

* * * * *

Our project in So Batatas in the Santo Elias community near Rio de Janeiro was partly the vision of Dr. Haroldo Neves. He wanted to do something about street children in the area, so his church identified 20 children ages five to nine and set out to help them. They first purchased a one-story house and remodeled it into living quarters for these children. We came in and constructed a second floor for a potato chip factory. (*So Batatas* in Portuguese means "just potatoes.") The children will be trained to make, package, and distribute potato chips to earn money for their school and living expenses. In this way, the children will be off the street, earning a living, and learning a trade.

Dr. Haroldo had once been a street youth himself in this area. Beloved missionary Jim Kratz took an interest in him. He got involved with young Neves's life and learned of his dream to become a medical doctor—a dream that had little chance of becoming a reality given his meager circumstances in life.

Rev. Kratz led Haroldo to the Lord, and the Nazarene church nurtured him in the faith. When he finished public school, the church took offerings and helped get him established in medical school. They could not afford to pay his entire way through his medical training, but the women of the church took Haroldo on as a personal project. They conducted fund-raisers across the years and helped as much as they were able.

Now this good doctor has returned to his community and established his medical practice there to pass on the blessing he once received. He carries a burden for the citizens of his community. That's why he wanted us to come and help get the new potato chip factory started. His personal interest was evident; he visited our work site every day between his office appointments and worked alongside us. Our team observed the tireless efforts of this committed servant of God, and they learned a valuable lesson in Kingdom priorities and investing in the lives of others.

Another long-term result came through the efforts of the Brazil health-care team. Students in the nursing and physician's assistants programs from several of the Nazarene colleges and universities joined together to form this team led by Dr. Pam Smith from MidAmerica Nazarene University. Dr. Haroldo placed them with Brazilian medical professionals and used them to form one of the best programs in the area for screening and preventing uterine cancer. The exam centers that they set up will assist many women in the future, and Dr. Neves is currently documenting the effectiveness and results of this program in an article for the *Journal of the American Medical Association.*

The C.A.U.S.E. work projects also gave the Brazilian Nazarenes new eyes to see the street kids of Rio. Up to this time they had not really wanted to work with this problem as it seemed too big and unsolvable. Rio has the largest population of home-less children in the world, and Nazarenes did not know where to start. They had been actively in-volved in working with "at-risk kids," children who seemed to be heading in the wrong direction with their lives, but they had avoided the problem of homelessness. Since the Americans and Canadi-ans returned home, Nazarenes in Rio targeted a ministry to street kids. Pray that God will continue to bless their efforts.

Argentina even got involved in the Brazil proj-ect. Instead of simply working with our team, young people from Argentina took this effort a step farther, formed their own work team, and came to work in Brazil. This was the first time that a youth team came from a country other than the United States, Canada, or the host country. The Argentine students studied the Brazilian project plans and team organization, and then they returned home to reproduce the effort there. This is another example of God using our efforts in ways that we coordina-tors had not anticipated. A silent revolution is cur-rently mobilizing the youth of our denomination around the world. Pray that God will continue to multiply these efforts and challenge youth to King-dom service.

I would readily admit that it costs a lot of mon-ey to transport and care for an entire team of work-ers in a foreign country. If our only accomplish-ments are building construction and remodeling, distribution of clothing, food and medicine, and a little evangelism, then the effort is probably too expensive. However, far more happens in the lives of both North American and national youth than meets the eye.

The long-term results are often staggering. North American youth are given firsthand exposure to the work of missions. National youth are given firsthand exposure to the skills and talents of North Americans. All have their cultural and spiritual horizons expanded by each other. They learn to work together across cultural and language barriers. They have their eyes opened to a new, larger world with a bigger view of life. They challenge one another to seek God's call for their lives. And they give God an opportunity to set circumstances into motion that take the work farther than anyone realized it could go, like a ripple effect from a stone thrown into a pool of water. So long after the last team goes home, the work "keeps going and going and going."

Chapter 7

The Big Picture

I HAVE HAD THE PRIVILEGE of being involved in C.A.U.S.E. from the beginning, and its entire story represents an amazing miracle of God's direction. C.A.U.S.E. did not begin in one of the offices of World Mission at International Headquarters for the Church of the Nazarene, nor in a faculty committee meeting on one of the Nazarene campuses, nor in the mind of a missionary on the mission field. C.A.U.S.E. began in the sensitive hearts of average, ordinary college students who heard the voice of God and responded. No doubt, they had no idea at the time the far-reaching impact of their beginning efforts.

The date was April 1985. The place was Trevecca Nazarene College (now University). The event was Nazarene Student Leadership Conference (NSLC). NSLC is an annual gathering of student government leaders from all of the Nazarene colleges and universities in the United States and Canada for inspiration, information, and a cross-fertilization of ideas. Students come and learn and then return to their home campuses with a direction of leadership for the coming school year.

A group of students at the 1985 NSLC carried a particular burden to get more involved in ministry to the hungry, poor, and needy in other countries.

They saw the skill, energy, and ministry that college students had to offer, and they wanted to see that force tapped for the kingdom of God. A resolution passed in that conference to discover ways to involve college students in ministry to world areas.

At the same time, God dealt with a college student from Trevecca named Kevin Ulmet, who approached Dr. Mark Moore, then international commissioner of education for the Church of the Nazarene. He asked him, "How can college students do something to help the hurting and hungry of other lands?" Dr. Moore was impressed with Kevin's enthusiasm and contacted Dr. Steve Weber, international coordinator of Nazarene Compassionate Ministries (NCM). The two men determined to find a way to use college students on the mission field.

Two other college students, Bill Sunberg and Doug VanNest from MidAmerica, attended the 1985 NSLC and were challenged by the call to compassionate ministry. God gave them a dream to see MidAmerica students put together a Work and Witness team, so they contacted Rev. David Hayse at the international Work and Witness office. "We don't want to wait for all of the research and studies to be conducted. We want to get involved *now!*" they said. "Can you find us a project on the mission field *this year?*"

Rev. Hayse had just begun his Kansas City assignment and did not know the organizational ropes yet, but he later told me, "I was so impressed with their youthful enthusiasm that I just had to help them fulfill their dream." He gave them the green light on a project in Tegucigalpa, Honduras. These two college

MidAmerica Nazarene University's first C.A.U.S.E. team in Honduras.

students took the initiative and contacted the mission field. They even worked out a funding plan. They stopped by my office one October afternoon with a request. "We need a faculty sponsor to supervise us. Will you do it? We'll do all the work if you and your wife will just give us direction and travel with us."

Sue and I didn't have the heart to tell them that college kids are too young and inexperienced to tackle such a big dream. After all, God gave it to them. We sensed God directing us to do it, so we jumped on board their venturesome effort.

Bill and Doug modeled our work team after a local church or district team and modified it for a group made up entirely of college students. It had never been done quite like this in the past, so we weren't sure how to proceed. We built our wagon as we rode in it, so to speak. All of the Nazarene colleges and universities had taken faculty-sponsored groups of students to the mission field. This experiment differed, however, in being completely organized and operated by college students.

This first effort had to fly. A successful trip would pave the way for future ones. Failure might end it all. We had one shot at it; we needed God's help, and we knew it. God has blessed C.A.U.S.E. beyond our wildest dreams.

*　*　*　*　*

By the time you read this, C.A.U.S.E. will be beginning its 14th year of service. This book has attempted to offer a thumbnail sketch of the program and its impact. Too much has happened with too many people involved and too many lives impacted to give a detailed account. This is a continuing story; as long as humanity suffers desperate need and God calls college students, chapters will need to be added to this account.

Through C.A.U.S.E., college students learn compassion as a lifestyle and as servant leadership. They realize that no matter what their skills or interests might be, God can use them to minister to people's needs. Exposure to international ministry and involvement in cross-cultural opportunities give participants a global perspective. Once a heart for ministry is created or nurtured, they usually seek ways to be involved in ministry on a daily basis at home. C.A.U.S.E., then, impacts both impoverished communities for Christ and each person involved with a life-changing experience.

The field coordinator logging the most hours working with C.A.U.S.E. teams is Duane Rensberry, missionary to Nicaragua with his wife, Linda. He worked with the two MidAmerica teams to Honduras and all of the campus teams in Costa Rica and Panama. Duane has a clear understanding of the mission of C.A.U.S.E. He offers this perspective on the program:

"C.A.U.S.E. is great! When I think about it, my head spins with all the work and energy it takes to make it work smoothly. At the end of each group, when we meet to hear the testimonies of the college youth, my heart rejoices. I thank God, for only eternity will reveal the complete tally of results."

Duane and Linda have lived in Central America for 13 years. They see the great human need and the inability of international and governmental organizations to meet it. But they believe that God can bring hope and renewal through students like those who come with C.A.U.S.E. "Our youth need to see that the answer our world needs comes from the Church. Only Christ can change the hearts of people and, one by one, change a nation. Coming from a society of self-sufficiency, the cross-cultural experience of C.A.U.S.E. is of utmost importance for today's Nazarene college youth. Advertisements bombard us with ways to pamper ourselves, but C.A.U.S.E. helps us to see and respond to the needs of others. C.A.U.S.E. gives 'mission vision.'"

"Mission vision" is the essence of what has captured the hearts of our students. Year after year they go on the trips dedicated to helping those in need. Year after year they return radically different young men and

Missionary Duane Rensberry enjoys an evening meal out in Costa Rica.

women. The stories of Jon Kroeze, Jon North, Brian Watson, and Larry and Phyllis West highlight those called into full-time mission ministry through C.A.U.S.E. A mighty host of other C.A.U.S.E. students also serve full-time on the field: David Allison in Albania, Jay Sunberg in Russia, David and Hillary Balsbaugh in Malawi, and the list continues. Brian Schaffer, Cary Murphy, and Fred Warkentine will follow soon.

"Mission vision" manifests itself in a variety of ways among our graduates. Melody Haller taught school in Haiti until the overthrow of the government forced her return. Candi Cook served two terms in Papua New Guinea. She returned to the States for a couple of years and has since returned to Papua New Guinea. Beth Bustle, one of our nursing graduates, took the initiative to get several of her nurse friends together for the past several years and form their own medical missions teams to Guatemala. More than a dozen of our students have led their own work teams to the field.

"Mission vision" has certainly caught on at our house. We have witnessed the profound impact the C.A.U.S.E. trips have had on our family life. True, the trips do create stress in the weeks immediately preceding and following the annual trip. And our family has never had a spring break of relaxation since we began teaching at the college. But the mission vision of C.A.U.S.E. is worth the costs. We would not trade the impact of these trips on our family for the world.

Our son, Brent, started going with us when he was nine years old. Over the years, he developed a sensitive heart to the needs of others and Kingdom priorities. During his senior year in high school, he wrote an essay, "Giving to Others," demonstrating the impact of C.A.U.S.E. upon his life. It is reprinted here with his permission.

Giving to Others
by Brent Moore

Warm, humid air mists against my face as I am awakened from sleep. Yelling noise from the street corner grates obnoxiously, more so because it is in Spanish. (I am in Tegucigalpa, Honduras.) Every year my parents take a group of college students to a foreign country to build houses and churches. It is spring break, and this is an interesting way for a third grader to spend it.

I step off the bus at the work site; the sun's rays

burned without mercy on my face. A variety of tools and construction materials stared at my childish face. The task before us seemed impossible. We begin work for about two hours constructing a church building. My throat is dry and my shirt wet. Sweat covers my body, soaking my shirt as if I had been swimming. "Ah, swimming, that's what I normally do during spring break. So why am I here?" I grumble to myself. I am about to figure that out.

Finally, the time came for a work break. "Time for snacks," said someone. It seems an eternity for this time to come. I take my snacks, cookies, and am about to take a bite when I noticed a boy sitting close by. I will never forget his face; his name was Victor. He sat there in his ragged worn-out clothing, which I'm sure were all he owned. Suddenly, a war explodes in my head. Should I give my cookies to him or keep them for myself? The breakfast we had wasn't much, and my stomach growled at me with discontent, but his hungry face fixes my eye and diminishes the contest. I walk over and give him my cookies. His dark hand reaches out, and he jumbled sounds; there was a language barrier, but we still communicate through our expressions. At that moment a special feeling came over me, a feeling I had never experienced before. It was the satisfaction I felt inside for helping him. As I watched him eat, I noticed for the first time that giving really is better than receiving. Is it any wonder why my parents do this annually? It isn't for the suntan or the recognition, but for that good feeling of helping others.

It's been about nine years since that experience. I've found many ways around our community to help others, such as working at the Kansas City Rescue Mission. The Rescue Mission is close by, but the need is still the same as in Central America. I can remember prying open the rust covered, bent up cans at the Rescue Mission kitchen to help serve those less fortunate than myself. I also help others by gathering cans in canned food drives that our church holds. I go door-to-door asking people if they would like to donate any nonperishable items to the needy. All of these kind doings I attribute to that warm, humid day in Honduras.

* * * * *

To this day I remember with strong emotion a lecture my church history professor presented while I was doing graduate work at Vanderbilt University. He was discussing the student volunteer movement of the late 19th century. He told of the vision of John R. Mott and Ralph Speer as they visited colleges and universities across the land, recruiting student volunteers for missionary service. He painted the picture so clearly I could almost see those 811 students step forward at the end of a Nashville rally and dedicate their lives to full-time Christian service. I will never forget the cry of my heart that day in class as I prayed, "Do it again, Lord. Send us another student volunteer movement for our generation."

Little did I know as I sat in class that day that God would someday let me have a small part in just such a movement. God spoke to a number of students more than a decade ago, and they responded. He has continued to speak down across the years since that time, and students continue to respond. The future of student involvement in the work of missions is as bright as the call and vision of God for their lives.

This generation of students and young adults has been labeled generation X. They are called this because they seem to stand for nothing and believe in nothing. They seem to be committed to very little and refuse to get involved in the world at large.

But I work with generation X every day, and I can honestly tell you that the Christian young people I know are not typical generation Xers. They stand for the cause of Christ, and they are ready to commit themselves to the advancement of God's kingdom. Students of this generation have seen the bankruptcy of their culture. They know that mass media and the glitter of culture do not satisfy the deep longing of their hearts for fulfillment. They have realized that you do not find yourself by looking for yourself but rather by giving yourself away in service to others in the name of Jesus Christ. They are turned on by this realization, and they are enlisting their peers to join them in record numbers.

The challenge of the Church of the Nazarene, as never before in our history, is to harness the wind of the Spirit as He blows through the lives of young people. They are giving themselves away in service to Christ as they further God's work of missions in our world. They are showing us what God can do with anyone fully committed to Him. And they are proving the truth of Paul's admonition to Timothy: "Let no one despise your youth, but be an example to the believers" (1 Timothy 4:12, NKJV). May we all have such "mission vision."

In Memoriam

I have dedicated this book to the life and ministry of my friend Charles Morrow. He's gone, but the work he loved so much continues. Hundreds of people, both American and national, are impacted; buildings are erected; souls are won; needs are met; lives are changed by the power of God. I often think of Charles as we see the accomplishments or spiritual victories of a particular C.A.U.S.E. undertaking. The following quote from Jason Shaw's summary paper following the Rio trip is fitting tribute to the impact of Charles's ministry:

> There was a man by the name of Charles Morrow; I never met him, but I wish I could have. Because of this man's love and obedience to Christ, my life was changed. As Thursday night's service came around, a few of the people we met on the streets and visited at homes showed up to worship with us. For one man, it was his first time to come to church. That night after talking to a couple of other students, he accepted Christ for the first time. Charles Morrow could have never known that his obedience to Christ would eventually lead a man to Christ in Rio de Janeiro.

Scores of souls have come to Christ throughout Central and South America because of obedient college students. No doubt, Charles is smiling down from heaven right now and in his characteristic way saying, "See, I told you—no problem!" Thanks, Charles, for your mission vision of C.A.U.S.E.

Charles Morrow assists students with money exchange in Guyana.

Charles Morrow family at the dedication of the church built in his honor in Liberia, Costa Rica.

Appendix

C.A.U.S.E. MINISTRY LOCATIONS

1986	Honduras
1987	Honduras and Guatemala
1988	Belize
1989	Guyana
1990	Costa Rica
1991	Mexico
1992	Panama
1993	Dominican Republic
1994	El Salvador
1995	Venezuela
1996	Brazil
1997	Belize

CAMPUS C.A.U.S.E COORDINATORS

Canadian Nazarene College—Ms. Colleen Smith
Eastern Nazarene College—Ms. Amy Zimmermann
MidAmerica Nazarene University—Dr. Frank Moore
Mount Vernon Nazarene College—Rev. Joe Noonen
Nazarene Bible College—Rev. Earl Wheeler
Nazarene Indian Bible College—Mr. Charles Stuart
Nazarene Theological Seminary—World Mission Fellowship
Northwest Nazarene College—Rev. Gene Schandorff
Olivet Nazarene University—Mrs. Donna Lovett
Point Loma Nazarene College—Mr. Scott Shoemaker/ Mr. Dana Walling
Southern Nazarene University—Mr. Dee Kelley/ Ms. Nancy Stewart
Trevecca Nazarene University—Ms. Julie Stevens

Notes

1. Oh well, since you asked, the custom throughout much of Latin America recommends placing used toilet paper in a trash can as sewer pipes are not large enough to handle the paper. Not seeing a trash can, our flight mates opted for the rest room floor. A stream of water from the leaking ice bin ran under the bathroom door and soaked everything. Enough said.

2. One night when we ate dinner in a Belizean restaurant, the server informed us that the two items of choice were rice and beans, or beans and rice. Apparently rice and beans are mixed together, and beans and rice are served separately on the plate. Keep that in mind if you ever order a meal in Belize.